This book was written to promote Positive emotions, belief and resilence in children.

It is a book that parents, carers and role model adults can lead a child through.

This book is all about reminding a child of who they can be and who they are at their best.

At the end of the book youll find some blank pages for the child to create their own personal positive messages

The "I AM" Experience

Dedicated to my wonderful
husband, Andy and our beautiful boy,
Stirling Fox.
May you always know that You are
Special, you are Amazing and you are
Loved. You can achieve anything!

I AM....A Book about me

Written by Kate Marshall
Illustrated by my little amazing helpers

Copyright 2022 Kate Marshall

First printing 2022

Published by ingramspark
www.theiamexperience.com.au

ABN 81797518921
ISBN 978-0-646-85898-2

The "I AM" Experience

I am....

This is my story

Being Loved makes me feel
safe and happy.
I am loved by many people,
most of all,
I Love Myself

Can you name someone
who loves you?

I am Loved

mark 6 years

when I am kind,
it makes
others feel special

when did you last show
kindness?

I am kind

scarlett 6years

My mind is as strong as my body

How do you exercise your mind and body?

I like to learn and practice new skills

what is one thing you have learnt today?

I play and share with my friends.
I look after them,
and they look after me

Who are your friends?
How do you look after them?

I am a Good Friend

Bronte 8years

Everyday, I find something
to be
Thankful for

what are you Thankful for today?

I am Grateful

Emily 12 years

Even if I am scared,
I try
my very best

when did you last show
courage?

I am Brave

Elliot 12 years

I know the difference between
Naughty
and
Nice

what is an example of being Honest?

I am Honest

sofia 11 years

I keep my body active
My mind curious
and I eat my vegetables too

How do you stay healthy?

I am Healthy

Leo 11 years

I may not always win
Or be good at everything
however
I always try

DEscribe a time when you had to put
in extra effort

I am
always trying my best

Riley 10 years

Being in the moment
Soothes and relaxes me

How do you Relax?

I am Calm

Rose 10 years

Sometimes Im Happy
Other times Im Sad,
and sometimes
Im inbetween.
I know how different
feelings feel.

How are you feeling right now?

I am
In Tune with my
Emotions

Jessica 8 years

I am

There is no one else like me

I am
Special

Grace 8 years

Pictures from my special little helpers

Bowe
12 yrs

Now it's your turn

I am...

I am...

www.ingramcontent.com/pod-product-compliance
Lightning Source LLC
Chambersburg PA
CBHW040250100426
42811CB00011B/1211